REMEMBERING FRIENDS

poetry *Pt* today

REMEMBERING FRIENDS

Edited by Suzy Walton

First published in Great Britain in 2001 by Poetry
Today, an imprint of
Penhaligon Page Ltd, Remus House, Coltsfoot Drive,
Woodston, Peterborough. PE2 9JX

A Catalogue record for this book is available from the
British Library

ISBN 1 86226 623 9

Typesetting and layout, Penhaligon Page Ltd, England.
Printed and bound by Forward Press Ltd, England

Foreword

Remembering Friends is a compilation of poetry, featuring some of our finest poets. This book gives an insight into the essence of modern living and deals with the reality of life today. We think we have created an anthology with a universal appeal.

There are many technical aspects to the writing of poetry and *Remembering Friends* contains free verse and examples of more structured work from a wealth of talented poets.

Poetry is a coat of many colours. Today's poets write in a limitless array of styles: traditional rhyming poetry is as alive and kicking today as modern free verse. Language ranges from easily accessible to intricate and elusive.

Poems have a lot to offer in our fast-paced 'instant' world. Reading poems gives us an opportunity to sit back and explore ourselves and the world around us.

Contents

Remembering Friends

A friend is someone that's there
whatever the weather.

A friend is someone that's kind
and understanding.

A friend is someone that shares
your happiness and sadness.

A friend is someone that shares
your tears and pain.

A friend is someone that shares
your smiles and laughter.

A friend is someone like you.

Valerie Gaynor

To A Special Friend

Today would have been your birthday my friend, born 1921,
Oh, the tales you used to tell me, of your childhood filled with fun.
When friends and neighbours, you said, were 'the salt of the earth ~
giving support to each other for all they were worth'.
But life wasn't so kind when you were grown up,
it seems you were destined to be down on your luck,
left on your own with three children so young,
you worked really hard to make their childhoods fun.
In the evenings, for friends and family you would knit and sew,
in the daytime, off to work in the factory you'd go.
Your life wasn't easy, I remember the tears,
but you gave them your all through their growing up years.

When the children were married, the grandchildren came,
you welcomed them all and loved each one the same.
But then life for your son wasn't going so good
and you found yourself raising 'a second brood'.
With the grandchildren grown, great grandchildren bring you
new joy,
two pretty girls and a handsome boy.

Then, once again, you were down on your luck,
as sadly, we learned that cancer had struck.
Though you were terrified, still you would joke,
of this monstrous thing invading your throat.
So cheerfully and bravely you fought, it seemed you had won,
but it wasn't to be, now my dearest friend is gone.
I'll cherish your memory till the end of my days,
For your big kind heart and your selfless ways.
There could be no finer soulmate under the sun,
than, you, *my special friend,*
My own dear mum.

Eve Gibson

Cherished Memories
(Grandad this one is for you. I hope you can read it from Heaven)

Always in his same chair,
wooden and covered with brown.
Sat lightly, never hearing
but always listening!
'Who's that? . . . Don't know her.'
Then, back to puzzles,
jigsaws and crosswords.

Still I remember
those strange little things.
Slurping hot tea,
taking control of the telly zapper
and falling asleep. Then saying
'Who me? . . . I was awake all the time,
I was just resting my eyes.'

Always there to meet a challenge,
maths homework his speciality.
How he'd puzzle and work things out,
never ceasing to amaze.

People would jest. Here today gone tomorrow,
but I never really thought it could be true.

But now, there's no more tea slurping or telly zapping,
maths homework or tales of the past.
Just wonderful memories,
of my white haired loving Grandad.

Amanda Clapp

What Midlife Crisis?

For unnumbered years you've weathered life's storms
With admirable persistence and graceful form

From my observations of your persevering ability
Your future poses few problems for one with such agility

Fortunate I am to enjoy your friendly relation
I anticipate much joy through its duration

Having observed your style for quite a while
It is indeed no surprise for me to surmise

That you must be made of pretty durable stuff
To have survived so well through times so tough

Happiness be with you in this the prime of your life
I wish for you many years of absence from strife

My desire for you in all sincerity
Is a life of good fortune and prosperity

Mary Cathleen Brown

Christine

Her name was Christine; she came round to play.
School holiday time she came every day.
She was gentle and sweet and never cross;
She let me play Teacher or Nurse or Boss.
I showed her my dolls and brand new kitten,
A Persian Blue; Christine was quite smitten,
And she was there, I did not need to say
How sad I was when he ran away.
When two baby birds fell out of their nest
We tried to save them, in vain did our best.
Christine was with me, we both sat and cried
The evening those poor little fledglings died.
I showed her where pink flowers grew by the pond;
She met the ponies, of whom I was fond.
Her hand clasped in mine, we strolled down the lane.
I told her my secrets, my joy and pain.
I made up stories to make Christine laugh.
How frightened we were when a cow ate my scarf!
We looked for violets beneath the hedge,
Heart's ease and pimpernel at field's edge.
Our days together were sadly numbered,
Those years when we wandered unencumbered.
We drifted apart, I needed her less;
Other play-mates visited my address.
There was home-work to do, pop stars to chase,
Pass exams, get ahead, join the rat-race.
Christine disappeared, just came to an end,
My dear little imaginary friend.

Verity Poole

Dedication To A Friend

You went away so suddenly
I couldn't help but cry
But now I know that you are safe
I can heave a relieving sigh.

It hurts to know you died alone
I keep asking myself 'Why?'
Now as I come to terms with my grief
I just want to say goodbye.

You were such a special friend
The kind that's rare and true
My grief will ease as time goes by
But I know I will always miss you.

Lynn Kilpatrick

The Twins

The twins' birthday is here again.
Which is a special day that's plain.
They have feelings that no one knows.
Their friendship is so strong and no moans.
It is hard to tell the difference in many
twins that is true.
But it really makes a difference
in many twins that is true.
But it really makes a difference they love
each other through and through.
They like to have the same presents,
They always dressed the same, but one
in pink and one in blue. And nothing else at all.
They have a special kind of love that no one else
would ever have, or even know.
All through life they have had theirs
A bond wherever they go,
But sometimes they need the closeness
that we will ever know at all.
And to know where their other half is
or to give a little phone.

Heather Breadnam

Remembrance Of A Happy Friend

The day is dull, it is November,
Dark clouds are full and I'll remember
The thin grey haze of falling rain
That meets my gaze through the window-pane.

Tenseness is in the air ~ a sudden flash,
Silence everywhere and then a crash,
As thunder rolls and lightning gleams
And rain pours down in steady streams.

Across the sky a rainbow springs,
High and dry a blackbird sings,
A sudden gladness fills the air,
Gone the darkness, all is fair.

This transformed scene it is not new,
So it has been to have known you:
As that bird could not resist
The lovely rainbow in the mist.

So you brought 'midst toil and care,
A glimpse of sunshine everywhere,
Cares and troubles weigh down never,
A bounding spirit lives for ever.

Whenever there are skies of grey
I'll think of you then straightaway
The clouds will go and there will be
The sunny road you found for me.

O Miller

My Friend

A real true friend is a precious thing
They will support you all through thick and thin
No matter what the problem be
They are always there for you, you see
They laugh with you and share your joy
Or provide a shoulder on which to cry
They give all in sacrifice and love
Reflecting the image of God above
When you need help and time is short
They are by your side without a thought
To have someone with which to share
Whom you can trust beyond compare
To know that you can bare your soul
And know it's safe what you have told
In today's world instant and fast
We need a friendship we know will last
Can you be special to someone like this
Filling their life with heavenly bliss?

Veronica Quainton

A True Friend

All kinds of friends never seem real,
They'll say hurtful things, which make a big deal,
But who is that person who's simply the best,
Who gives you some help when you're in a big mess?
That person who brightens up your dull day,
They surely can't be real, that's what I say,
Well I know someone, who truly is kind,
She's got great taste and a sensible mind,
A friend like her is meant to be,
You'll soon find out and then you'll see,
This person has to be my Mum,
She is my one and only number 1 chum,
I'm very proud to have her as my friend,
We'll stick together until the end.

Natalie Hillson

My Friend (My Husband Ron)

When we met, all those years ago,
I knew at the time I loved you so.
We were together for forty-four years,
I never thought it would end in tears.
Our children, and their children,
are all that is left,
with great grand kids, who are the best.
You've gone to the Lord, and time will tell,
when I join you, up there, you will love me as well.

Val Nichols

A Teenage Friendship

They say opposites attract.
I was the class swot,
Wendy was the glamourpuss.
I buried myself in books, anything
For a quiet life. It pleased the teachers
And my parents, but not my classmates.

She was into boys and glamour, long
Before anybody else had the courage
To admit to having a boyfriend.
But she didn't care, she was in love;
The others could laugh all they liked.

An unlikely pair, but we gelled.
We confided our problems, and giggled.
I was far too serious, burdened with problems
I didn't dare share with anybody else because
In those days you didn't.
A choleric, shell-shocked ex-army Sergeant was not right
For a phlegmatic girl missing her real father, even if he did
Mean well.

Wendy and I would giggle our way through breaks,
Joking about the teachers and talking about marriage.
It loosened me up, gave me the chance to be a teenager.

In return, I listened and sympathised, and kept her secrets
To myself. She had difficulties at home too,
'Though different to my own, and I could empathise.
We've lost touch since, gone our separate ways,
But I'll always remember the confidences and,
Most of all, the much-needed laughs.

Kathy Rawstron

Snodgrass And Shail

Eithnée Snodgrass and Nona Shail:
One was rubicund, one was pale;
One was short and the other was tall,
But which was which I cannot recall.

Memory fades as the years go by.
One was extrovert, one was shy;
One was blonde, the other brunette:
Which was which? I quite forget.

One was fair-haired, petite and frail ~
Was that Snodgrass or was it Shail? ~
Pallid, retiring, rather a loner:
I think it was Eithnée ~ or was it Nona?

One was the life and soul of the party,
Gregarious, voluble, hale and hearty,
Raven hair, rosy cheeks, statuesque body:
I'm sure that was Shail ~ but it could have been Snoddy.

Their names still ring in my ear like a bell:
Shail and Snodgrass ~ I knew them so well
In the May of my life, but now it's December,
And which one was which I just cannot remember.

Robert Reeves

Tess

Across the miles
Across the sea
I know my friend
Is there for me.

Although we live
So far apart
She's always here
Inside my heart.

So thank you Tess
For being there
To share a laugh
And share a tear.

Across the miles
Across the sea
I know my friend
Is there for me.

Sarah Bell

You Were Born To Sail On Silvery Seas

You were born to sail on silvery seas
Coast the skies like a morning sunray
Spread your wings and fly with the gentle breeze.

Sing with a nightingale high in the trees
Glide on a moonbeam over the rooftops
You were born to sail on silvery seas.

Glowing in the wisdom of Socrates
Surfing the ripples of a dancing stream
Spread your wings and fly with the gentle breeze.

Voyaging the passing seasons with ease
Glistening brightly in a starlit sky
You were born to sail on silver seas.

Flutter in a rainbow of fallen leaves
Cruise on the plume of a floating cloud
Spread your wings and fly with the gentle breeze.

Maybe I'll cry but I will not grieve
When the dawn chorus ends and a new one sings
You were born to sail on silvery seas
Spread your wings and fly with the gentle breeze.

Maura Rea

Dedicated To Sheila

I have a best friend for 15 years.
We lived beside each other
Through trials and tears.
We had children to look after,
Sheila was always there,
To wash up or cook or just a chat,
I miss her so, I moved to
England and the pain was so awful.
Without Sheila things were bleak.
A good friend like her is so hard to find.
I'm living in Ireland again
Alas away from my best friend.
But I never will forget the good times we had
And I will never forget her.
Sheila.

Davina Glaser

The Embrace Of A Friend

How do I find the wealth of words
    To say goodbye to you dear friend?
For you have been the branches of the vine
    That fed me with words and prayers.
You warmed me with your welcome smile
    And the gentleness of your embrace.
We've sipped a glass of your country's wine
    Over words when you taught me how to pray.
And led my thoughts to find that peace
    Even where the flowers play.
For in nature's face is God's own hand.
    For in your hands even flowers talk.
For through your creations
    I found the inspiration for daily prayers
And all the richness that lies there within.
    So although I'm leaving, my spirit remains,
For when I hear the clock strike seven,
    No matter where I be,
I will always know, at that time, we are one
    In sharing prayers for each other.

Dave Flanagan

A Special Love

I will never forget, the day that we met
as my life from that day changed forever
Because the man that stands near, holding me dear
is the man whose kind love I will treasure
Forever untold, your heart I will hold . . .
your secrets and troubles for all time
And as we walk on life's path and grow old
I'll be with you forever entwined

Tracey Klenk

Wedding Belle

I hadn't known you long
Must've been less than a year,
But you and I just 'clicked'
From the beginning it was clear.

Whilst standing in those pews
Silent, excited nerves were felt,
Still, I was unprepared for
Just how you'd make me melt.

If hearts could skip or hop or jump
Mine would have won awards,
You radiated the entire brigade
As him you walked towards.

Draped in finest silken threads
Delicately touched by lace,
Causing smiles and tears alike
With such an air of grace.

In true Princess style, your fairytale
In us so magically entwined,
You proved a perfect picture
Of Angel and Queen combined.

Joanna Williams

An Ode For Auntie

Dear Auntie Anne I think of you
In oh so many ways,
Just little things that make me smile
And lighten up my days.

Beans on toast, egg custard,
Blancmange and trifle too,
Seaside trips and large ice creams,
All happy times with you.

And then I start remembering
About the things you did,
To brighten up the days back then,
When I was just a kid.

You'd tie a string around a jar
For us to go off fishing,
Make windmills from our comics,
Just like the best magician.

You'd fold a strip of paper,
Nothing very grand,
And cut a line of paper dolls
All dancing hand in hand.

You knew the cure for all our ills,
And bandaged up our knees,
Nothing was an effort,
You always seemed at ease.

Sometimes on Sunday evening,
On a bus we'd hop,
And take a ride to Flackwell Heath,
For nuts and crisps and pop.

Twice a year on the 'workman's',
To London we would go,
To shop for spring and summer clothes,
Or warm things for the snow.

The things we did, the fun we had,
When days were always sunny,
We didn't need expensive toys,
Or yearn for lots of money.

Well now we come to visit you
For scones and cream and jam,
And talk about the old times,
Thank you, dear Auntie Anne.

Joy Rolls

I Once Had A Black Horse

Caress of a kiss
or a thousand whips
that touch of the wind,
earth racing beneath my feet.

Pounding of thunder
thudding the ground,
volcano of steam rising
heating the air.

Treacherous grip
of sand moving,
slipping, holding, held
in the damp spray of the sea.

Quiet in the lull before battle,
lonely
in that moment
when the battle is lost.

I once had a black horse
dark as the night
warm as the sun
part of my body
part of my mind
fierce as a lion
steady as truth.

Pam Redmond

Remembering Friends

I went to Singapore the year 1961
And had a very happy time indeed
With new found friends and fun
Three years we lived there
Found plenty of things to do
Involved in lots of parties
We went on trips with views
When we returned to England
With friends we keep in touch
Keeping our friendship blooming
Because they mean so much.
We just had a holiday
With two of the special ones.
However our hearts are broken
Because life dealt us an awful blow.
In the last three years the other two
God decided you had to go.
It makes our lives empty
And fills us with sorrow
But maybe one day we will meet
On 'time's up' Big Tomorrow.
In the meantime life goes on
With our loved ones and family
Who fill our lives with love
For whom we thank the Lord above.
It's at times like these we like to make verse
It fills us with ease as our sorrows we nurse.

Jean Broadhurst

Shirt

Washed so much its clootie* soft,
Vague blue checks diminished with love,
Torn and abused, with tatty collar and cuffs.
Indulgence is given to its threadbare state,
Whilst comforting children at night, late.

Filament cloth with Venerable thread
Persona hides well its younger affability,
It's been through labour and laughter
Posed sexily (in its younger days).
Taken on funerals as years fade.

Once worn only on halcyon sky days
Now only washed on bright breezy blue days
When its nightly return is greatly guaranteed
Redolence clings to my second skin,
As sleeping securely I'm smothered in him.

*Clootie: Scottish word for a child's security blanket

Stevie Mackenzie

Lost Time

Where did all the time go?
All our time we had together
Seems to have drifted away;
You're nowhere to be seen today.

Wish I could find you again
To relive those happy memories;
You're all I ever wanted in life,
Only one to ever brighten my days.

Sarah L Grigor

Sour Sorrow

Where did you fly to, friend of mine,
When finally you flapped your world-wise wings
And flew, away into the yawning space of death
Whispering through pain filled wasted lips, why?

Did last night's thinning air prove adequate
To hold up wings of God alone knows
How much, how little, faith in
Whose God alone knows what?

Did life's experiences, lessons learned, unlearned,
Provide the means of crossing over from
This vague and floating island of our thoughts
Into the realm of fixed reality?

What did you find, or what found you?
Was there some crashing cosmic echoing thunder
Waking your dreamed of sleep of death, or
Warming rays of some celestial sun?

Rather the worship-worthy windlass of our souls,
Which, weighed down with wandering this waning life,
Are wound towards the Word, the well-loved Son,
Who whispers, 'Welcome, wearied wakeful one'.

Where did you fly to, friend of mine,
When finally you flapped your world-wise wings
And flew, away into the yawning space of death.

Andrew G Phillips

Remembrance

In days which first appear to be very bleak
And friends are often difficult to seek.
You recall those days that used to be,
When new friendships made life so very rosy.
Remembering those friendships made so freely in younger years,
Will always help to wash away any fears.
As days go by you may lose many,
And not venturing forth each day find it difficult to replace any.
However true friendship will never die,
For there will always be those happy times ~ which mostly
                                            dormant lie.
We can relive those days ~ time and again,
And from most unhappiness refrain.

Betty Green

Hungry Birds And Children

When the earth is covered white
   And lakes are traps of silver,
Winter speaks like painted dreams ~
   Without the woe of hunger.
(Never a dead robin on a Christmas card)

Mercy is man's amusement
   As he feeds the hungry birds;
'Was this not God's intention?'
   Is his boast of loud-mouthed words.

Death-drenched India in the sun
   Living time in hated-heat,
Jubilance to them is water
   And to children rice is meat.

Man of Mercy do not waste
   People's time with crumbs of bread,
For whilst you dither payment
   India's race is falling dead!

T Graham Williams

28

The Old Soldier

Until I was five years old, a photograph was all I had
For me to look at everyday, of my dear soldier Dad.
He was so very far away you see, along with many more
Brave and courageous soldiers in the Second World War.

When the long awaited day came, I knew him straightaway
And ran down the path to greet him, and begged him to stay.
All through my years of growing up, he would not say a thing
Of what happened in the jungle, when fighting for the King.

He was such a kind and loving man, and popular with all
He loved to watch the cricket, and the local football.
But still he never mentioned the days of long ago
How he and so many others must have suffered so.

Then when my Mother died, he came across some poems he'd sent
Along with letters that reminded him of just where he went ~
All those many years ago, and the memories came flooding back,
And he started to relive those days when everything seemed black.

He started to write a book about the war time years
And he described just where and what were his many fears
Of his many exploits in the theatre of war, and then
Especially in the jungle, as one of Wingate's forgotten men.

The book was then published. He had finally told his story
And put the past to rest, it was now consigned to history
This account of one man's war and how it shaped his life,
Because of the poems kept for fifty years by his beloved wife.

When he died as a final tribute, to this old soldier so brave
As the curtains were gently closing the words the vicar gave
Were the words written by my father to finalise the book ~
'The day will come when the order to fall in is heard
And all we old soldiers who are left will quietly and slowly
                                        march away'.

Jo Robinson

29

Ghosts
(Dedicated to George Ralph)

Out of sight, yet not of mind,
A memory never left behind,
As through this life I make my way,
I hope that by my side you'll stay,
Unseen, but not unnoticed,
You are always in my heart,
If I could turn the clock back,
I would never let us part,
With so much left unspoken.

I took your love for granted,
When it never was denied,
But since the day I lost you,
Through the oceans I have cried,
I find that all I've wanted,
Is to see you if I might,
And yet my mortal blindness
Hides you from my sight,
While my shattered heart lies broken.

But on this long and dusty road,
I'll journey not alone,
A faithful friend will guide my steps,
Until I reach my home;
Although a place I know not yet,
A place of endless peace,
You'll be there waiting at the gate
Then all those words I left unsaid,
Will never go unspoken.

Sarah Maclennan

The Friendship Of A Postman

My friend he was a postman
Whose name was Alec Black
He walked down the street, each and every day
With letters in a sack.

I got to know him very well
Both bachelors were we
We would holiday together
To country, or to sea.

We would often visit the local
For a pint, as we stood by the bar
Talking of things that we had not done
Like going to places from afar.

But suddenly, Alec passed away
It is sad for me to say
His friendship will always last with me
Until, my dying day.

When he gets to heaven
St Peter will look around
Here is your post sack Alec
This is your final round.

F King

31

Anne
(July 1999)

You have been a dear friend to me
Listening through thick and thin.
I sometimes wonder where I'd be
Without you somewhere in my life.

You have been friend, companion and adversary
In a fickle world that I fail to understand.
Your constancy and belief in me
Has given me faith in myself.

At first you scared me
But then I came to know you.
You have so much to give
And many who appreciate you, I suspect.

Who knows what lies around the corner.
Maybe it is best we don't know.
We know little of acceptance, you and I
Yet there is an acceptance in that.

I fear what lies ahead.

Annie M Rawsthorne

Remembering Michael

I miss your laugh
The jokes you told
Your sense of humour
And heart of gold.

I miss your good nature
Your sense of fun
Spread all around
Touching everyone.

Each person knew you
In different ways
With shared happiness
Brightening up their days.

Life was brighter
With you as a friend
The light is dimmer
Now it's come to an end.

Sheila Graham

Mission Impossible

Relationships, Friendship, Whatever!
The warmth and touch of a friendly kiss
To place our arms around each other,
Is not unusual when one likes another,
But what should happen when attraction stales?
When the feelings we have fostered
Seem to have faltered and failed,
When our dreams have gone sour,
And castles are crumbling by the hour.
How do we know what the other is thinking?
Are we so sure that the friendship is shrinking!
We try to be careful, to be diplomatic,
Always aware that care is erratic,
We think of the time when our friendship was strong,
Then wonder and worry, what the hell has gone wrong?
What do we do when we are in this dilemma,
For checking on something so important as this,
Is not always careful and not always clever,
So how do we test if a friendship is forever?

Bah Kaffir

A Song For Love To Return

Touch my life, my love
again
touch and let the loving flow.
Share my life, my love
again
share and let the caring show.

Now less selfish, less demanding,
now more tuned to understanding.

See my life my love,
see it's wanting without you.
Be my life, my love
again
be and let us live for more.

John Ellerton

Anne

You came from afar
To rescue me
From loneliness and sadness

With your gaiety and your sayings
'One thing leads to another'
'Even the beautiful have to go'
~ made me smile ~ and ponder

Anne of the red hair
And entrancing walk
Anne of the skill with words
And the fascinating talk

You came from afar
To rescue me

John Dossett-Davies

Shalom
(Peace be unto you)

Safely by his Father dwelling,
High amidst the Cherubim,
And the Lovely One beholding,
Looking unto Him;
Of the Holy Spirit learning,
Midst the Seraphim.

Surely as each measured heartbeat,
Hushed his earthly life away,
Apprehends he now the Secret,
Learns the Mystery,
Of the Word of God incarnate;
Man of Calvary.

William Mead

Memories

In the hazy half world
Between sleep and waking,
Myriad mixed up memories
Flit in and out of my mind,
Like random images
Projected on a screen.
In sunshine and shadow
I see two girls,
Talking, giggling, laughing,
Playing, sharing, learning,
Sisters from choice.
No Lissadell gazelles these,
But raw boned and lean,
One frame crowned with rich red hair,
The other taller, plainer, more unsure.

Two faded ladies of uncertain age,
Lunching, laughing, talking,
Relating their lives,
Reunited: the teenage bond unbroken
Fifty years on.

Jean Blayney

To Joyce

You are the sister that I never had,
You've seen me through good times and bad.
We know each other so very well
You guess what I'm thinking before I tell.
I truly believe we were meant to meet,
Friends for two decades that's no mean feat.
So I cherish our friendship, dear friend of mine,
Being together was God's design.

Hazel Ratcliffe

Daydream

My life's a journey by Nancy.
Contents page ~ whatever you fancy.
Holidays abroad, trips afar,
flights to Venus, Pluto and Mars.
On my travels the sky's the limit
anything's possible with me in it.

Where today? I hear you wonder,
intrepid explorer; the wide blue yonder
beckons with extravagant boasts,
ample opportunities, welcoming hosts.

My fantasies forming, growing
developing; knowing
that's just what they are.
Express lane, a ride in that car
of imagination. Give me room
watch out ~ mind that boom!
Faster than a speeding bullet
Quick grab that line and pull it!

Got to go, have to dash,
do interplanetary stations dispense cash?

Sarah Allison

Mum
(Aug 1910-Apr 2001)

I've lost you now, dear mum and friend,
Your life has come to a sudden end.
You've been with me since life began,
A 'great grandma' ~ a loving 'nan'.
You lived for us, you were always there,
So special we could ne'er compare.
You scrimped and saved, gave us the best,
We were not rich, but nicely dressed.
You never saw us go without,
You were so special there's no doubt.
You gave us love, you cared so much,
The special smile, a mother's touch.
We loved you then, and love you now,
We'll ne'er forget you anyhow.

There was no sign or any warning
You closed your eyes, but you weren't yawning.
Your body tired, you couldn't go on,
The pain you suffered for so long.
You wanted rest, you wanted sleep,
You closed your eyes so very deep.
You knew we wouldn't mind you leaving
Your body frail, with gentle breathing.
We watched you go, we said goodbye,
We couldn't help but start to cry.
Your life had come to a sudden end,
I miss you mum ~ my 'bestest' friend.

Liz Ryan

My Adopted Dad
(Dedicated to J Tetstall)

The only friend I ever had.
Happened to be someone else's dad.
He looked after me when I was small.
Respect myself, and make me feel tall.

He was the only dad I ever had.
As my own father left, because of
Drink and getting mad.
He's not just my friend.
My protector, my hero.
Thanks to his care, everyone else is a zero.

Now God took him away from me.
And in my heart, he'll always be.
No-one else will take his place.
Or let me forget his loving face.

So when I feel sad and blue.
I think of him, and the laughs, we knew.
If some-one you love has gone away.
Remember you'll see them again some day.

Mary George

Christmas Past (A True Story)
(Dedicated to my wife Angela)

Christmas time should be full of fun,
A happy time for everyone.
But spare a thought for those far away,
Not with their family on Christmas day.
Like those in hospital getting better,
Or the ones who can only say
'Merry Christmas' in a letter.
I look and see the snow all around,
And deep in my memory I have found,
The sight of a child with wonder on his face,
And of his sister so full of grace.
When he woke and saw his presents
His eyes bright and wide,
He looked at his amount
Then to his sister's laying there by her side.
My wife nearly cried when she saw his eyes
As she stood by the door,
It was plain to see that he couldn't see
His other ones on the floor.
But he was quite happy
With the amount he thought he had got,
I can tell you from my heart
The look on his face will never be forgot . . .

Bill Bogan

Pure Skill

Fine young Will Shakespeare often must have found
The going rough as with a supple quill
He penned his verse, depending on his skill
With words and syllables alone to sort the mound
Of thoughts and notions teeming through his head
And turn them into sonnets. No quick aid
From thesaurus or dictionary swayed
His choice of phrase: he'd have to spread
Across his table rhyming words in lists
To end each splendid line he wrote to tell
His lady of his love. The numerous swell
Of well-schooled reference books that now exists
Was not to hand. Yet clever Will could set
A standard way past anything I can get

Frank Littlewood

Arms Open Wide

Our friend Barbara is a dear
When we arrive ~
She comes down her drive with her arms open wide
With welcome and love in her blue eyes.

Over the years she has always been there
She's known all around
For her kindness and care
No one is ever turned away ~
It's open house every day.

Now everything is changed
She's ill and needs our help
People turn up from all around
With flowers and love abound
Their arms open wide for her!

We talk to her on the phone
So that she will know she's not alone
Although her husband too is there
For her *our* arms will always be open wide
We hope that God will do the same
If he decides to make his claim!

Sylvia Jennings

Forever Diesel
(To a special canine companion)

Your amber eyes no longer shone
The dance within your step had gone
And each day as the warm sun rose
I watched the tiredness in your pose

My darling dearest loving friend
I never dreamt your life would end . . .
So soon, and on the blackest day,
'I love you' was all I could say

You'd only reached your second year
I can't believe that you're not here
I'll love you Diesel till I die
And everyday I'll wonder why

How can it be, 'Life's so unfair'
You seemed to say as you lie there
And as we said our last farewell
I caught a glimpse of living Hell

My days are empty and so blue
And every waking thought's of you
I'm sure we'll meet again one day
And from my side you'll never stray

Please wait for me in your new home
Enjoy the green fields that you roam
For one day I will join you there
And stroke again your golden hair

Until that time please have such fun
Race through the grass, laze in the sun
In my life you took the starring part
And you'll stay forever in my heart

Joanne Wood

Friendship
(Dedicated to Henry)

You're the kind of person
That I would like to be
You've touched my life in many ways
And mean so much to me

A caring heart when days were dark
And seemed to have no end
Someone to share my golden days
Thank-you for being my friend.

Bess Langley

Friendship

Friendship is a bond so great
That sees no end
Or fears no fate
It thrives within the depths of man
Seeking to find a friendship span
Friendship found compares no cost
But it's never valued until it's lost
For this state of mind
Is a happy relief
It may be long
Or it may be brief
But to know that somewhere
In this lonely life
There is always one
Who shares in your strife
Your thoughts, your deeds
Your every whim
Somewhere, somehow
Are safe with him

Fiona Franklin

AFC

He was a kindly unpretentious man,
Devoted to his Maker's plan,
A friend of all in every village,
Their hope in pain or lack of privilege.

When two or three met together,
He shared the light that lasts forever,
Until at ease all went their way,
Once more renewed for many a day.

A single suit, an ageing pipe,
His enquiring manner shed delight,
His hand oft' held a Dickens treasure,
He knew them all and had their measure.

He loved to fish in any river,
Ne'er missed the float's slightest quiver,
No Summer heat or insect bite,
Could take away his sheer delight.

A friend indeed and sorely missed
His essence ever will exist.
In these lines how plain to see,
Glimpses of immortality.

L J Harries

A Sonnet For Mary

Mary, at ninety-three years, is a true human being and friend
An epitome of womankind's good qualities which never end,
She reaches out with understanding and gentleness,
Knowledge, love and exceptional kindness.
A caring mother watching her family growing,
Nurturing, teaching, beseeching, bestowing
Undaunted by any adversity encountered,
A lady of culture, grace, well-bred,
Polite, refined, keen of mind
Who has lived longer than most of mankind,
Passes on her knowledge to colleagues each day
Learns something new, a different way ~
Mary is my mentor, a wonderful friend,
With her, new heights we will both ascend.

Floriana Hall

Grandad

For 88 years his life span ran,
Never once calling his fellow man.
His grievous suffering so bravely borne,
He now dwells with the Lord, leaving us forlorn.

His well kept garden was his delight,
He worked in it morning, noon and night.
Chrysanthemums and roses his special loves,
Now he tends his garden in heaven above.

His wife and family were his treasures,
Horses and cards some of his pleasures.
On the railways, he walked miles each day,
People needing help were never turned away.

We shall miss his wondrous smile,
His love of talking with all for a while,
His joy in Nature, the heather, the moors,
He was happiest out of doors.

Our lives were enhanced by his being our friend,
We shall love and remember him until our life ends.

Ruth Malton

51

Legacy Of Hope
(For Philip)

Tomorrow I want to know that
I will remember yesterday with pride,
I want to know that as I found my way
I learned to feel sorrow,
If only yet to know I found the sunrise.
Tomorrow I want to know I learned to cry.
I want to hold the memories
of those who ask but why?
For once I walked where few
would ever go, saw some things
I'd ne'er forget, some sights that haunt me so.
For once upon my yesterday I learned of hope and will.
Tomorrow as I stand upon the beach
help me to remember that I taught a soul to reach,
forever to the fields where they'd run,
if only but to shed a tear for the blessings time had won.
When last my time has come to walk away
let me see the rainbows o'er
the storm clouds of my day.
Let me know that last I chose to be
but a moment in my brother's life
and the hands that set his free.
For once upon so long ago I learned to live
with sorrow, in the hope these hands of yesterday
brought sunlight on tomorrow.

Kim Davenport

Bereaved

Gone
Gone where?
I know not, but I pray
For him
For me;
Separated.
A free spirit, no pain
A new world.
For him, I hope
For me, I weep
Grief is real, unrelenting
Like the sea in waves
Washes over you, engulfs you.
And yet, I feel you near
Encouraging, cherishing . . .
Now I can smile at the memories
Rejoice in a life spent together
A life lived well.

Alison Watkins

Remembering

You skipped towards me,
Brightening the playground with
Your tomato-red coat,
And your smiles.
Nothing pastel about you.
Fun and intrigue drew us close
In, 'let's pretend' days;
Escape from rage filled houses.
Time shifted us from play to work
And screen gods to drool over.
Life drew us apart.
But now and then the soft tone
Of your voice
Would speak my name
And I would turn in Woolworths
Or the street,
To see your blue eyes dancing.
I heard you joked about losing a breast,
But you were claimed, not by illness
But by a driver's mistake.
I remember you with your special smile
That said, 'I am your friend.'

Kathryn Graham

A Good Friend?

'Am I never to see you again?'
My life will turn into oblivion.

'Are we not having the time of our lives?'
Please don't disappear without a trace.

The magical aroma you release,
Makes my world a better place.

'Have we not climbed mountains and reached stars?'
Please don't let go and break my heart.

Chandra

Friendship

True friendship is a treasure,
A gift beyond compare,
Of worth, beyond all measure,
So handle it with care.

True friendship is a haven,
Wherein two folk can grow
in difference, yet in freedom,
True liberty still know.

True friendship never stifles,
But opens up the way
for visions and attainment,
It welcomes, come what may.

True friendship brings the sunshine,
When dark the clouds may be,
A lifting of the spirit,
A life line, given free.

True friendship spans the barriers
of every time and place,
It's forged, not forced, no dictates
of colour, creed or race.

Take it for granted never,
Abuse it not one time,
For once the cords you sever,
You'll lose that gift sublime.

Jeff Hancocks

Poem To A Friend

Just Jean
Jean is my best friend, she lives across the miles
We used to have many happy beautiful smiles
I had to come back to my homeland
Right back in England but she is grand
At picnic point a barbecue and a chat
No longer can we do that
I remember Boxing Day
The family all met, a happy moment to share
Food prepared with love and care
Two weeks ago we had a meeting
Although brief I send her my greeting
Get well soon and good luck.
One day we will be back
And we will share those moments again
And no more will there be pain
All love to our friend
Poem's end

Frances Dyke

Bags Of Swagger

Her Majesty's Footguards,
The finest in the land,
Heads held high,
Tears of pride, glinting
In their eyes.

Bearskins combed and groomed,
Tunics red as blood,
Boots shining like mirrors
In the sun,
They march together sounding
As one.

Battle honours won at cost,
Guardsmen's lives have been lost,
These are the men you
Will never see,
Who fought and died to
Keep us free.

Tourists gathered, on the
Street,
Bandsmen playing, listen
To the beat,
Men marching on to glory,
The world is at their
Feet.

Wayne Cotter

Friendship

Friendship should last. Its value's like gold.
It cannot be bought, it cannot be sold
And as life passes by its journey to wend,
We're never alone, there's always a friend.

Friends may not agree as ideas come along
When thoughts of the one to the other is wrong.
Disagreements may come, that is often the way
But friendship goes on for ever and a day.

Troubles may come and troubles may go
Often they pass but sometimes they're slow
But one thing we know and on that we depend
We always can turn to a good honest friend.

Trevor Gilbert

A Sprig Of Time
For Sheena

For a few brief hours
we wandered through primrose woodlands,
past murmuring streams,
garlanded by willows
and sprigs of thyme;
singing snatches of folk-song,
wearing shoes of fine green leather
Down by the sally gardens
overlooking *Afton Water:*
the land of Burns and Yeats.
Trees rustled through the churchyard
and far away
a lark sang in the clear air
as time stood still one summer day.
An afternoon remembered, savoured;
its fragrance lingers:
a sprig of time.

Penelope Freeston

I Remember . . .

I loved an old house, once ~
   and will again ~
I loved it in all weathers
Wind and rain,
The hot, sweet kiss of summer sun
The gentle twilight of days gone.

I loved it as a part of me
And hear, again
The sighing wind, the tapping vine
Against the window pane . . .
The many times I lingered on the darkened stair
And listened to the whispers on the midnight air.

Too soon, too swift, the child became the man.
Will ever the ghosts forgive
The carefree smile, the manner of my going?
My hands reached out for more than they could give
I shut my eyes to all that I held dear
And turned away the memories of yesteryear.

I remember when my love was all
Fast, embedded, deep . . .
I feel the beauty and the sorrow stirring, still
Within the troubled, tangled hours of sleep
And when ~ in pain ~ I try to draw myself apart,
I hear the throbbing of the lonely, aching heart.

As wheeling, calling seabirds
Under a winter sky
Cutting their sharp, grey crescents with curving wings,
Always, I hear ~ insistently ~ the far off cry
The distant pleading voice . . . 'So long away . . . so far away'
Oh yes, I know I will ~ I will go back . . . someday.

   Joanna Carr

61

Christ, The Sacred Heart
(For Jeremy RIP 19th May 2001, age 24)

Given for us
Yielding to all
So that love might come in:
A young man lies dead
He was humble of soul.
Strew his way with flowers
That he might still be
Servant of all there in Heaven.
And forgive him
    if he strayed. Amen.

Peace be with him.

Hazel M Smith

Softly Fallen
(To Brenda with love)

Pastel, that's how I think of you,
Not brash tomato red or vivid blue.
No you were soft, like a kissing breeze
And you were fun, and you could tease.
But best of all you were my friend,
And still you're close. That has no end.

E A Kibbler

Remembering Friends

'Remembering friends after they have left this life
Sometimes it is said they are at peace in this world of stress and strife.
We remember those dear friends who have passed away
And recall happy times spent with them on many a day.
Good friends today are not easy to find as we know
So we should return our friendship and let it show.
Do we value as we should those friends far and near
Do we let them know how much we care and do we make it clear?
Alas, we do sometimes neglect our friends and that's not fair
We should always show that for them we care.
Let us then reflect on our good fortune by having friends
If we have forsaken them in anyway we must do our best to
                                                    make amends.'

Peter E Parbery

As Free As A Bird

Where are you now, you're no longer here,
Are you with Rosa, together you cheer,
Are you now free, free from all pain,
A happy peaceful soul again,
Like you once were, before you got ill,
When time ticked on and never stood still,
I hope you are free, as free as a bird,
No-one to stop you, you'll never get hurt,
I'll try to be strong,
And accept that you're gone,
But in a way you'll always be here,
Your spirit, your soul will always be near,
Deep in my heart, that's where you will stay,
No-one can touch it, can't take you away,
Lorna I love you, you are a great friend,
I will not say were, cause our friendship won't end,
I'll love you forever that will not go,
I'll never forget you, I'm sure that you know,
I can't wait to see you, I miss you so bad,
If I die early I'll truly be glad,
I'll see both my friends, but happy and free,
That moment I'll cherish and can't wait to see,
Your angel like faces I can see clear,
My memories of you I hold very dear,
I find it impossible to say goodbye,
When I've so many questions, like how did you die,
I'll try to be happy for you now you're free,
But I wish one last time your face I could see,
I wish I could hug you goodbye,
I wish you didn't have to die.

T Davison

In Memory Of Scott
(28/6/98-19/3/00 ~ best friend in the world)

A theatre ticket stub ~ a memory
A photo ~ more memories
Songs on the radio, voices in my head
Replaying conversations from the past
Loaded with memories.
Hard times shared together
Good times enjoyed
A shoulder always to cry on, hands to pick up the pieces
And a sense of humour to make me laugh ~
Such an amazing sense of humour!
And courage, such incredible courage
Living the dream
Enduring the pain
Always thinking of others
And us forever changed
By that impact on our lives.
And now no more pain
Freedom and eternal life
Young forever, laughing and happy
And smiling down on all of us
In approval of our lives
Still taking part, still caring
Always there.

Kirsty Donald

Rendezvous

Stolen days . . . hidden and secret
The passions burn and smoulder on
Stolen nights of love and longing
Remained within me, tho he had gone.

Days of fun and conversation
Nights of love and holding near
Remain to fill my waking moments
Even tho he is not here.

Oh, how the hours now move so slowly
Until I see him once again
Soon, my love . . . we'll be rejoining
Even tho it be in sin.

So helpless, now . . . to push back the feelings
That I have for him alone
A former lover re-enters the present
Bringing forth past love that again has grown.

Remembering initials carved so many years ago
Sharing old memories . . . and, the new ones made . . .
Reliving the feelings we had felt then
Sharing hours together . . . as each day fades.

How will we part, when our time has ended?
And, oh, what tears will surely fall . . .
Saying goodbye will surely fell me
For this man who is my all.

How will I leave you? How will I say goodbye . . .
Once our days come to their end?
I cannot imagine being without you . . .
I'll love you always . . . my lover, my friend.

Mary Beth Bott

67

Tears On My Pillow
(Dedicated to my only love, Gerald)

Behind my smile there lies endless, countless tears,
What can happen now to allay my fears?
It seems a lifetime; we parted three hours ago,
My love, my darling, I wept when I saw you go.

We are so much in love, do not forget,
The story of our romance when first we met,
Remember when we looked into each other's eyes,
My life is now full of a thousand sighs.

You promised we would meet again, and said 'do not cry',
I said to myself life can be cruel, I ask 'why'?
I stretch out my hand, you're not there,
Tears on my pillow, 'where are you, where?'

The love that we have, may it never fade,
We must embrace and nurture it, love must be obeyed,
Love will be our strength, comfort and our guide,
It is in our hands, my darling, only we can decide!

Irene Greenall

I Thought You'd Live Forever

I thought you'd live forever
Or that's what I believed
Now I'm what the Doctors call;
One of the bereaved

I never got to hold you
Or tell you of my love
Now you're sitting on a cloud
Somewhere up above

I still hold my tummy
Sometimes it feels like you're still there
I never got to hold you
And show how much I care

There'll never be another you
A babe to love and hold
There'll never be another you
From this body so empty and cold

Gillian Morphy

To My Friend

Have we been friends for seventy years
How can it be so long?
We have shared so much along life's way
Our hopes, our plans and our fears.

Early years at the infants school
Which we knew and loved so well,
Then off to the 'juniors' up on the hill
With games in the Bunny ~ for good or ill!

That memorable day we had a fight
Who 'won' will never be known.
But we came to our senses and started again
With friendship replacing the feelings of pain.

So to you, dear friend, I give you my thanks
For the years together we've shared.
And I give you a toast by pigeon post
May the Lord bless and keep you and those you love most.

Barbara Evans

You're The One

One day when I'm weeping,
Your heart will be bleeding,
This sole dream is forever sleeping,
Nothing is ever what it seems,

One day my wife,
The next a new life,
Sweet love listen to this story,
So gentle and unknown thoughtless glory,

Your stunning looks,
Another page in your long lasting book,
Pick up the phone I do,
If you're not there I'll cry for another day,
Or the girl that does care, I'll find another way,

The day I met you,
The day I saw you,
I knew you were the one,
Until the day it's over,
Then I wish you'd fly away as far as you can see,

My life such a mess,
Your loving much a test,
So on bended knees I beg you,
Say you'll be my only faith of true love,

The past is no more,
The future is never complete,
The heat of the moment is yet to be decided,
Twisted memories amount to poor communication,

You're the one,
My petal I thought,

Gary Thompson

Last Request

My tears were warm, your face so cold, your lovely smiling face so
still.
I had to let you go, as you asked me to.
Your final words 'Don't hold me back for tho' I love you it is time for
me to go'
I thought when all else failed, that if I held my body close to yours, I
may ease your laboured breathing.
I thought I was the strongest one this time, but you knew best, I had
no part to play.
In your last battle you fought and won the day, a part of me went
with you when we said goodbye that day.
Tho' I am sad and lonely, tears never far away, I will keep our golden
memories, safe and warm in my heart.
With the knowledge that I let you go
    I played my part
        I loved you so.

Ivy Woodward

In Memory Of A Lovely Lady

She was my inspiration
    she treated me with care,
though she herself was far from well
    with burdens hard to bear.

She always said that God was good.
    Her heart was filled with love.
She never said an unkind word
    and she always understood.

Though she's been gone for several years
    I still think of her with love
and imagine her gazing down at me
    from up in Heaven above.

Her name was *May*
    and I rue the day that she left us all alone.
For she was one of the nicest souls
    this world has ever known.

Val D Warner

My Friend

Will you be my friend as the years unfold,
Bringing whatever they may?
Be it good or ill will you be my friend still,
And share our love as today?

Many years we have known one another,
Joy and sorrow together we've shared,
Each knowing whatever has happened,
There's a loving friend who has cared.

As along life's journey we travel,
We cannot see round the next bend,
And though we might stumble and falter,
There's the warm loving hand of a friend.

Pauline Brown

Fading Photographs

At rest inside a spider-ridden room
with edges curled and here and there a crack,
some photographs are lying in the gloom
with images in sepia, brown or black.

Each sentimental pause is distant now
as like an insect in a chrysalis,
I peer through space to wonder how
I can forget the friends I used to miss.

We were conventional and knew our place
but I was longing to be free
and hardly recognise the dismal face
in photographs my mother took of me.

The 'maybe' and the 'might' are in the past
with years of emptiness between the hands
which hold me now to show that love will last
and those who held them then on golden sands.

The secret bond of friendship always stays
consistent in an ever-changing world.
But distance brings a parting of the ways
and leaves the flying flag of friendship furled.

Communication ends. Birds fly the nest
and photographs are left to gather dust.
I treasure one or two but leave the rest
for those who follow on to hold in trust.

Nancy Reeves

The Three Musketeers

Another new term, and
any sadness dissipates as each of us arrives back to our home
                                        from home.
Screams, hugs, a whole summer's gossip; ten to the dozen.
We three. Brought together by circumstance.

Popstars, posters, magazines, films,
parents, shopping, bras and boys.
We sit, laugh, eating biscuits, drinking coffee,
and vow never to grow old.

In our retreat, sparsely furnished and decorated by *Just 17,'* ~
together we learn of rebellion and fun.
Stumble through first romances and heartbreaks ~
Work, play and sleep, 'One for all, all for one'!
and vow never to grow old.

Another bank holiday, and
any tiredness dissipates as each of us arrives to another's
                                        mortgaged home.
Screams, hugs, months of news; ten to the dozen.
We three. Brought together by friendship.

Husbands, holidays, music, shows,
children, work, waistlines and memories.
We sit, laugh, eating salad, drinking wine,
and vow never to grow old.

   Sigrid Marceau

Our Gran

Each little piece cut out with care, of cotton, lace and print,
Then sewn together carefully, arranging every tint,
For it is grannie's pride and joy, her patchwork cover gay,
Recalling bits and pieces of bygone yesterday,
The velvets and the satins, vie with stripes and spotted cotton,
And with them come the memories, which ne'er will be forgotten,
And as Gran thinks back o'er the years, her eyes all misty grow,
How bittersweet her memories are, of days so long ago,
Dear Gran . . . She knows of aching hearts, . . . enjoys her
pleasures too,
She gives her love unstintingly, her love is just and true,
If you would be just like our Gran, forget yourself always,
Serve others far less fortunate, be happy, all your days . . .

L Page

Memories Of Keith

We met you and Trudi thirty years ago
When ballroom dancing was rife
Then you emigrated to Shelter Island
With American Trudi as your wife

We corresponded, sent photos
The thought of visiting brought a glow
Two years later we departed
With four children in tow

The wildlife was amazing
Right away we felt at home
From Shell Beach we collected shells
Pretty dogwood everywhere we roamed

Our children's eyes were like saucers
When they saw deer and a racoon
Then we set off for New York City
By coach we arrived at noon

We viewed Manhattan with awe
Eighty-six floors up the Empire State
Broadway, Times Square, Liberty Island
The children couldn't wait

In UK we laughed on the phone in the morning
We made plans to pick you up on Sunday
Little did we know dear friend Keith
That day you would suddenly pass away

We will treasure all of our memories
Of last October spent with Trudi and you
At beautiful peaceful Shelter Island
With our friend we loved and knew

Diana Cramp

Reflections

In the depths of the earth
Everyone has a very special place
A secret of some kind
Like a sound passing through water
A teardrop of a ripple moves
Over the surface
Showing reflections of a face
That we remember
From our future from our past
Like the face of the moon's light
Transcending a path through the night
Like the smile of the sun's rays
Gazing through the visions in the day
From our childhood to our journey's end
We all need to recollect with stability
In reflections.

Matthew T Lindley

Angels Would If They Could

I'm an angel, I look out for lovers,
But I don't always win.
He stands in shadows in the rain,
Waiting as he always waits, scheming, dreaming,
Hoping for a sign from me, or a situation tailor made.
She, dream of delight, stands in a doorway bathed in light,
She wears a shiny raincoat and a see through plastic hood
Cowgirl boots and a wide red belt,
I'm an angel and I knew she would.

Was it reality, or was it a trick of the mind,
Maybe a sad healing lie,
But was there some message in the way she turned,
The slightest hesitation, a shrug of resignation.
And was there a small line at the corner of her mouth,
Not a smile, not even a half smile,
Just a softening, a line that said I'm sorry,
Sorry that you never thought, sorry that you never knew,
Sorry that you could not change that dreary part of you.

From way on high, I saw the bus was coming,
She ran around the shadows, shiny raincoat plastic hood,
Shadow man and sometime angel,
We always knew she would.

   Doug Smith

80

The Well

The cold slip
Of water over my hot wrists
Impels memories. They strip
Through accumulating winters

To the breathing flesh
Of that reviving spring.
The onrush
Of blustering days

Has not blasted the leaves
Of the secluded year.
They interweave

Arches for us as we lower buckets
To a well of cool limpidity,
In silence, fill.

Frances Gwynn

Postage Stamp

At the foot of the bed there's a long list of names
With a line crossed through every one.
It isn't a list of the women that I've had,
Because I haven't even had one.
It's a list of all the women I have known
Who never acknowledged my love,
Women who I dreamed would be happy with me,
In sharing our dreams and true love.
At the end of the bed there's another sheet of paper
With a list of the women who loved me.
And a blank sheet of paper for those that I missed
Where the time wasn't right or the place wasn't right,
Or I didn't know, or she didn't say.
At the end of my bed is a postage stamp
To stick on the letter to send to the woman
Who was there on the list of those that I loved,
And there on the blank page of those that loved me
Who I missed,
Yet I dream of,
As I lie here alone.

Robin Graham

82

The Old Folk Next Door

We have lived here some thirty years or more
We came when there was an old lady living next door
Our other neighbours had a family of girls just three
But very soon it was obvious there was another child to be

The old lady in the adjoining house
Finally became ill and died as had her spouse
Her house was taken by a couple of a mixed marriage
But quite some time passed before they required a baby carriage

In this house the family grew
Along came a baby girl, this now made two
As the children grew space became cramped and had to improve
So the house was put up for sale and the family made a move

It was soon bought and a young couple moved in some time ago
They have made alterations, how long they will stay I do not know
They are both pleasant and friendly as neighbours should be
They have no family yet but we will wait and see

I can't help wondering if our neighbours think of us so
As the Old Folks, just as we did long long ago
Time has changed our positions from those of before
Sad but true, we are the Old Folk living next door

John Nelson

Rose

(In loving memory of Rose Tuohy 1981-2000, rest in peace friend)

As beautiful as her name,
A rose, Rose,
Such a beautiful person,
Her memory will live long in our hearts,
I still can't believe she's gone.

As friendly as she was beautiful,
She had yet to celebrate her twentieth year,
Yet life became unbearable for her here,
All the people she left behind,
Miss her dearly.

As cold as it may be now,
I don't feel it anymore,
Without her all the lights went out,
So young, too young,
To end the life of an angel.

To look upon the warmth of her face,
Could make a person smile,
Or cause their heart to miss a beat,
With skin so smooth and eyes so bright,
That's why now, without her, it isn't right.

Shauna D Westwood

Old Friends

We forget about our distant relations, we forget about
our long time ago friends.

We say we must visit them one day, then we leave it
for another while and forget that time must sometime end.

Then we get a message one day, from a relative or your friend,
time indeed has run out, for your relative or your friend.

We feel sorrow, that time has run out for our relative or friend,
but then it does not matter now to them,
for indeed they have reached the end.

Now we remember all about our relative or our dear departed friend,
but it is too late now to renew old acquaintances,
with our relation or our friend.

Then we think about long ago friendships but still we do not learn,
although at the time, for their company we yearn.

Remember one day it will be your turn, for time will run out
and it does work two ways, they could have visited you,
before your time ran out.

Now there is always a chance that one day, that you may meet again,
but will they want to know you, they may feel you let them down
one time.

So perhaps we should not put off till tomorrow what we can do
today, for when we lose a relation or a friend, grief is the price
we must all pay.

Ronald B Astbury

Hari Mau

We knew you, dear Hari,
From kitten to grave ~
In youth a great hunter,
Both wily and brave.

Amazingly agile
Right up to old age ~
When your poor hips were stiffened,
You became a great sage.

You'd watch from the window
With narrowed green eyes,
Benign and resplendent,
Incredibly wise.

You always were funny,
Would not be left out ~
Would insist on attention
With strong feline shout.

We remember you now
As you were in your prime ~
A wonderful friend
To last beyond time.

Jenny Mullan

Remember My Friend

Red spotted green fields
Below starling flocks.
Valleys, hills, mountains
And pretty flowers.
We were young then and almost happy.

Nice memories, funny stories,
Outings, parties and many more.
We were young then
And best friends.

Remember the dark clouds.
The snow, the rain, the rainbow.
The fast runs to shelter.
We were young then
And now not more.

Sandy beaches, hot days,
Shells, seagulls and rough waves.
We were friends then
But now not more.

G Austin

The Life He Never Had

I can only imagine
how he spends his days now.
I picture him in a room alone,
a single room, with perhaps a bathroom,
specially designed to meet his special needs.
I picture him sitting
in a wheelchair by a window,
looking out at those who can walk
and aren't disabled as he is.
I imagine that time passes slowly,
monotony only interrupted
by meals brought by a nurse
in a starched white uniform.
I presume he's filled with regret.
He's now had many years to reflect on it,
to contemplate the chain of events
that brought him to this place,
a sheltered housing unit for the paraplegic.
I expect he wishes he was dead. I would.
I imagine he listens to the radio a lot.
When he has the energy,
perhaps he can read a book.
I imagine he watches television
or listens to music.
He may prefer silence.
I expect he's bored.
I wonder how often he's taken out.
I wonder if he still writes.
I would be only too happy to visit,
but he doesn't accept visitors.
He turns them away.
He won't see anybody.

It's a shame.
They're his only real contact
with the outside world.
Without that life will literally pass him by
and he'll wake up one day
an old man of sixty, seventy, eighty.
He'll wake up with nothing left,
except to reflect on the life he never had.

Andy Botterill

Beloved

You are my beloved, my beloved.
You are my cherished, my child.
You are my heart's desire, o heart's desire.
My autumn day, my hope forlorn.
You are my blessed, my blessed one, my openness to you I behold.
My waking cry, my sleepless thought,
My spring romance, my winter soul.
My desert storm, my hope forlorn, my even song, my silent one.
You are my energy, you are my power, o radiance.
You are my morning's thought, my night time call.
My harvest morn, my shapeless plan.
My belief at day's break, my doubt at day's end.
You are everything and nothing, all rolled into one.
You are my crescent, on the darkest day, my sanctity in time gone by.
You possess all by which I live, yet you have nothing that I need.
Your ideals are akin with the stars,
Your voice distresses all my thoughts.
By you, I light a torch unto the world,
By you, I breathe my every breath.
I have nothing that you have not given me,
Yet I possess all that I have taken myself.
To you I owe everything, to myself I owe the truth.
To heaven and earth I earn my keep, to hope, to cry, to weep.
In all that I know, and nothing that I love, I sacrifice my nothingness,
To you I give what, meagrely, I have not.
My heart's desire, o sacred desire,
My hope, on days gone by, in time to come,
My beloved child, my precious one.
My time has come, my day has passed;
My torch has been lit, my presence has been noticed,
My eagerness, in every moment, depicted.
My wishes for a day, make that a thousand days, digested.
My belief that all will have its days,
My faith in all that has and has not been.

My hope in future's discussed and decided,
My joy of summer's first deliverance.
To you, and not to any other, I give my all.
O blessed, blessed child, I give my all.
O beloved, I have nothing more to say,
For it has all been said and done.
O beloved, accept me as I am and always shall for ever be.
Beloved let me be me.

Simon Moralee

Valerie

Germany was very strong and took the world by storm
The war was going on, everything was getting out of hand
After the war when Germany was crushed by many nations
Thousands of Polish forces came to Britain to live
One of the soldiers met my sister Olwen, as is the norm
They got married as many others, when to stand
At the altar at the Catholic Church, an idea or notion
Poland mainly a Catholic nation, both of them had this belief
Later my brother in law, traced his daughter to America
Many thousands of youngsters were sent from their homes
From their homeland in Poland, they were shipped overseas
My sister's husband eventually got his daughter home to Beaumaris
Her name was Valerie, a beautiful girl it was a miracle
I met Valerie first when I got my leave to come home
I walked her around the town it was Beaumaris by the sea
We went and looked at the sights, we did not tarry
Valerie must have suffered while her father fought in the war
She had lost her mother previously, she was all alone
She could not stay in Poland; she had to go to a better country
America was where she was free and the lovely land of Wales
I served the rest of my national service and I was in the clear
I saw her when I was home the last time, later she was gone
Where is she now I often ask myself, is she still in this country
What has become of Valerie I would like to know, lately?
I remember her face it is so lovely, her skin was like silk
She left Beaumaris those years ago, nursing in Liverpool I believe
I have not seen her since, I wonder how did she make out
To bring happiness into her life, which she deserves?

R T Owen
A Beaumaris Lad

Friends

My bungalow used to be full of friends.
When I had my son and wife,
Now I have lost both of them,
I live a very lonely life,
No friends come to see me,
They really don't want to know,
I can go from Sunday to Saturday,
I don't even see a soul,
Some days I feel miserable,
Other days I feel invisible,
Also I feel my age of sixty-eight,
As my friends pass by my front gate,
The days are long and the nights are cold,
I'm invisible now I'm getting old.

Ron Sawyer

Bridge Of Life ~ Of Many Tears

There are many of us in life, whose Mother's words, are lightly
                                                thought upon.
But how they come back to us, the minute she's dead and gone.
Oh Lord please overlook discretions which I have slipped aside.
For the man's not born, we are erstwhile, remembering Eastertide.

Past smiles and tears are memories of wiser years.
To sit and reminisce with friends, that by natures will no longer be
                                                in the audience.
That nods with knowing smiles, or sit with nostalgic thought awhile;
But with looks of disinterest and vacant stares.
Past lives are not yet theirs, to those a journey just begun.

It's dream of Fame and Fortune that lures far and wide,
A mystery we need to fathom out, for our future and our pride.
This need to dream and build castles in the air,
Is a carefree youthful heart, one's guilt we will not declare.

In my quiet moments I sit here on my own, day and night.
My thoughts go back many years, to the people I have known.
Heartfelt tears yet to come:

To respect the serious words of wisdom, and walk the troughs of life,
Lift their eyes to others cries, hold a hand for those at journey end.
Rest awhile to see abuse of life and land,
See the savagery of the human race where all but the few are
                                                abandoned to keep pace.
Where man hates man for his faith, caress his head to console
                                                his mind.

Of evil deed left behind:

Will they that have just begun their journey
See this hatred subdue?
And all sit as one in reminiscence of their yesteryears.

There are times in our memory, we see the cosy home.
The memory of the hearth, its teapot of polished chrome.
The tears that were in Mother's eyes, her heart within her voice.
Oh, Mother, love of mine, you gave such good advice.

Family, friends and our neighbours who all have played their part,
with visits, gifts and flowers to cheer a lonely heart.

Now there's a great amount of water, run under the bridge of life,
I still remember the greatest piece told to me by my mother.
As she held bread of life.
Listen lad, you'll promise ~ if you're tousled of your hair.
You'll not forget hand down your head ~ remember ~ The
                                                    Lord's Prayer.

Many have passed on now ~ some you can't replace ~ especially
a loving Mother ~ with her happy smiling face.
Others who I've lived near ~ and shared their final pain,
Although they've gone, I carry on ~ though the memories
                                                    still remain.
The bridge of life ~ of many tears ~ here and there.

   Viv Lionel Borer

Rutter Falls

We visited together,
Oh what can I say,
You thought I was joking
When I suggested the way.

Oh no not over the wooden bridge
Or to stand on the grass side,
But straight through the water
To reach the other side.

Removing boots and shoes
Trousers rolled and tucked up high,
Into the water we went
To reach the other side.

I turned around to see your face
The expression you had
Was so funny to see.
A golden moment for us I believe.

A place in time
Never to be taken away
Oh you did make me laugh.
What a lovely day.

Gill Bell

Remembering Friends

I do not know a man
with whom I could share
an evening's sunset and
sit in silence with on
Newcastle's shore to listen
to the sea and hear what
we've been told so often
but never understood.
'Be silent and know.'
But I could with you.

Jack Clancy

Remembrance

Remember not you held my dying hand
And kissed the fevered dew from off my brow,
For that was then, and this is later now
When grief has run its course o'er sky and land.

Remember not the years of toil and care
When life was anxious with its restless pace,
Nor yet recall the pallid passing face
When, weary, you and I the silence share.

Rejoice for days when sun and smiles were warm
And love was day on day a constant friend,
When laughing children filled our lives with charm
And all seemed beauty with no distant end,
For time will heal the wound that bleeds today
And laughter will return and chase the tears away.

John Peaston

Tribute To Ralph

He came to Blandford Grammar School from serving George
                                                    our King,
He came with special talents in very many things;
A Biologist, an expert, throughout the whole wide field,
A Master, fully taking charge, great discipline he yields.

His drawings on the blackboard, were the very best,
A shame to erase them, but always a new test;
His House was St Davids, of which he was so proud,
He praised and supported, along with all the crowd.

Each year he played hockey, for Staff versus school,
His skill was there for all to see, always very cool;
The organ and piano, he played with poise and skill,
His duets with Mr Watkins, always gave a thrill.

His sketching, painting, crayoning, showed skill of highest class,
His Christmas cards and paintings gave great joy to all the mass;
His frank and forthright comments, some did not want to hear,
But respect and trust he earned, if at times he caused some fear.

Ralph is no longer with us, we mourn his very loss,
Our thoughts go to all the family, he was the lovely boss;
His painting of the Lakes, lives with me day by day,
His music, drawings, tapestry, will never go away.

John Paulley

Devotion

He only has to look at you, with those eyes so big and sad.
Your heart melts in an instant, even when he's been rather bad.
He loves to dig the flower beds and roll upon the lawn.
When you go to scold him, he looks at you forlorn.

His basket is in the kitchen, he is not supposed to roam.
But he'll be first at the front door, when the family comes home.
His fur and hair fall constantly, it's everywhere to be seen.
A telling tale of trespass, where he's not supposed to have been.

He can hear visitors approaching, for what seems a mile away.
He ignores you completely, when you tell him he must 'stay'.
With muddy feet he is down the hall, before you can reach the door.
His wagging tail greets everyone and he's forgiven, once more.

A woodland walk is his special treat, he loves to sniff and smell.
Never wandering very far, he likes to know you are there as well.
Your company is all he asks and in return he gives so much.
Undemanding trust and love for a word or fleeting touch.

The years passed by too quickly, he lost that youthful zeal
Our devoted friend is no longer here, to follow at our heel.
Coming home is not the same, no one to greet us at the door.
We'd give the world to see again, those muddy foot prints on
                                                    the floor.

Yvonne Granger

You

Like the sunshine
After a day of pouring rain,
You dried my tears
And made me warm again
And when I look back,
Look back through the years
I remember the brightness,
Not the pain.

Like a tree, you gave me shelter
From the summer showers
And offered sturdy branches
For my climbing hours.
We were not together all the time,
All the time, it's true,
But so many happy moments
They were ours.

There's a rainbow in the dark clouds
But it soon will go.
Leaves, flowers, rainbows, sunsets
Disappear, we know,
But love's enduring comfort
It will stay, will stay,
Touched by nature, yet within us.
Keep the glow!

Gloria Joice

Spirit Drifting In The Wind

When one is totally at a loss
Paint over with gloss
Pain and suffering goes
Love always shows
Should you be lucky at love
With hand in glove
Touch, smile, shows through
It's not new
Chemistry always works
Fits and starts and jerks
Happiness shines through
For me and you
Love is always around
If you dig in the ground
Those of us who drift in the wind
Touched, grabbed and pinned
Will never be split
Or get in it
Bluer or greener
Dedicated to the love of my life, Josefina

Anthony Higgins

My Best Friend . . . Un . . . Me

As a child I was shy and somewhat withdrawn
all hopes of friendship lost and forlorn,
until that day you came out of the blue
and a friendship just, blossomed and grew.

Like a guardian angel, all my battles you fought
leaving them all in our wake, and all distraught,
always there to lend a helping hand
my destiny mapped out as if, pre-planned.

And at the start of each, brand new day
my friend's beside me all the way,
and even at night, in my dreams he appears
as a white knight to banish all my fears.

Always showing maximum concern
never asking anything, in return,
an invisible shield that surrounds me
but . . . there's only one problem I can see.

It's that my best friend, lives inside my head
we're one and the same; it has to be said,
some call it madness this problem I've shown
but . . . I'll never be lonely, or completely, on my own!

J R Hirst

Heather

I laugh with her.
She shares my gladness and my joy
And makes me smile.

I confide in her.
Our conversations twist and turn
But never hurt,
They remain protected in our mutual safety.

I cry with her.
She shares my tears and fights my corner
When I cannot
And life's struggles seem unbearable.

I lean on her.
She buoys me up with confidence
When self-doubt creeps within
And helps me view reality through objective eyes.

She is herself
She is Heather.

Jill Wilmore

William, Precocious Only Child

School boys, completely unknown to one another,
drawn together as communal intake at art school:
my immediate jealousy at his pronounced expertise.
On weekly set homework, my quiet resolve
to out-do William, so evolving my own style.

All friends together at art school,
then living compounded by World War 2,
we anticipating due call-up, at a loose end
William's father deceased, his P and D business
needing urgent assistance.

So I joined with William ~ paints, brushes and ladders,
we soon passed through naïvety into tradesmen!
The local undertaker hired we two,
a complete external decoration required!
'Mind you,' he hints, 'I do weddings also!'

Acting on the hint we propose wedding white,
that whole end ~ block building, high virginal!
As Nazi war planes droned over
the neighbourhood in assured dread, 'A landmark!'
William now relieved at his father's demise.

The long war years we were worlds apart,
he, I learned, in India, painting exotic landscapes!
~ although he gained a war medal,
though we never discovered why.
But, now, more to the point.

Back again together, each of us separately teaching,
he meets my sister, low and behold!
He becomes my close brother-in-law!
Many years families together; sadly, sadly, her premature death
his mind breaks down, now irretrievable in a nursing home.

James Lucas

My Friends?

Where have all my friends gone?
We drifted apart.
A couple of special ones,
still next to my heart.

I'll always remember,
the things that we done.
There was plenty of mischief,
but always good fun.

We were always together,
we didn't stray far.
I wonder about you all,
and just where you are.

Remember our rope swing,
over the Lade.
These things were all special,
to me they won't fade.

Then we would gather,
up at the swings.
We had some great times,
our own special things.

We all stayed together,
for quite a few year.
These memories to me,
I'll always hold dear.

There was someone among you,
who, meant that bit more.
Thinking about him,
still leaves my heart sore.

Most of us are married now,
and gone our own ways.
But I wonder, if like me,
you think back to those days.

I wish we'd all thought,
about keeping in touch.
Because right now, I miss you,
all very much.

H Cruikshanks

Anne Of The Infinite Heart

She was already seated at my left
when I arrived that evening
for the workshop. Her smile radiated
from her heart and there was an openness
about her which crumpled my defences.
She was a vulnerable lady
one who empathised with others ~
an additional burden for the wounded mind.
I have wrapped my arms around her
and she me ~ exchanging fortitude
and understanding. She is the Light
which softens my hardened heart
but now miles separate these
sisters of the soul. She's but a phone call
away and I feel her power when chaos
threatens to overcome me. We put on
our stiff upper lips ~ talk about trivialities
while loneliness cries quietly in the space within.
Our voices resound with responsiveness
enveloping us both with a recess from
habitual regressive thinking.
We never know when our tears will turn
into laughter but it does. It is the joviality
of release. Three cheers for Anne's rare
qualities. She is the Sun which sets each night
on the east side of Heaven leaving behind
her mark of ebullience and a smile lingering long
after the phone has been returned to its cradle.

Carmen M Pursifull & Edward L Smith

Song Of Love To Beloved

Dear love I never forget,
Your smile of great bright,
Opens my heart to the beat of your heart,
When two hearts meet,
Love becomes the greatest test,
Of great friendship of eternal effect,
Makes me sing of love always and cheer,
You the great friend ever,
My song of love never ends never,
Mornings and evenings my song my dear,
Has music very sweet,
To open your heart,
And sing a song for song,
An eternal mutual song!
An expression of love herald!
To all humankind,
To love and dance forever,
And sing for love ever and ever.

Jalil Kasto

Kurt

Do you remember,
That night not so long ago,
You saw the light,
And had to go,
Your loved ones,
Pleaded please don't go,
Your friends above,
Said are you ready now,
With a long look back,
You faded away,
So now you know,
What we don't know.

Karen Burke

Quiet Tears

I stand at the graveside and quietly weep,
For the friend that I had, who has fallen asleep,
For too short a life which has ended in pain,
And for me standing here, life will not be the same.
For all the good times, and the memories we shared,
And all through the bad times you knew that I cared.
You were troubled and angry with life at the end,
But we'd talk these things through, 'cos I was your friend,
And now your life's over, I hope you're at peace,
And the anguish and anger, has finally ceased.

Margaret Whitton

Furry Friends

Oh you are all cheeky monkeys
Come on now, out you go
I can't get by the fire these days
To warm my freezing toes

I suppose it's all my fault you know
I knew I'd rue the day
When I let you in to warm yourselves
I knew I'd have to pay

And all my lovely bedding plants
I wonder where they've gone
Mrs Brownlow gave them to me
I haven't had them long

You're always into everything
You've claimed the whole job lot
There's times I'd like to threaten you
With Mum's old stewing pot

But you know how much I love you all
And I could never hurt you
I just keep saying to myself
Patience is a virtue

Susan Olwen Papworth

She Who Helps!
(Thank you Abigail Burnside)

My troubles surround me
In a whirlpool of grey
Then you come
And wash it all away

Happiness comes to me
As your face cracks a smile
I believe
Our friendship can go the mile

You spend life being kind
Listening to problems
Solving mine
Helping others all the time

How can you be so nice
Laughter comes with that joy
Only if
You'd allow me to help

Repayment as friendship
Is what I have to offer
All you need
Is to agree to it

Rachel Cockerham

My Sister

'Now, hold her hand,' our Mum would say, whenever we went out
                                                    to play.
Then she would add, 'and don't forget', as though I could, she was
                                                    the Pet,
The baby of the family ~ my little sister, only three.
And so we trotted, hand-in-hand, into our Magic Garden, and
A journey to another world, a land of make-believe, unfurled,
Of Fairies, Giants, Gnomes and Elves. A land where only
                                                    we, ourselves,
Could be a part, or even enter ~ a Magic World, the very centre
Of our existence on the Earth ~ our innocence, our Universe.
A Magic World, where we could fly. 'Look, I'm flying!' I would cry.
'I'm flying, too!' she would reply.
And so we were, still hand-in-hand, flying in our Fairyland.

As years went by, we went our separate ways,
Yet still retained that bond from childhood days,
Shared memories of the years we spent together
Which, we both knew, would live with us forever.

Then came the call, not wholly unexpected.
I had been warned, and, almost, had accepted
The inevitable, bitter news
Of final illness, yet I could not choose
To give up on the slender hope, and pray
A 'magic' cure would yet be found, to stay
The closing of that door upon the day.

Then, 'Can you come? She's asking for you now.'
'Of course,' I said, not really knowing how,
But I secured a cancelled seat that day.
I called him back, and said, 'I'm on my way.
I'm flying! I'm flying! I will be there,' I cried.
'Thank you,' he said, 'I know you've really tried.'

She died before I reached her ~ and ~
I was not there to hold her hand.

Jeanette Haxton

Mum

There's a light always shining
when darkness descends
radiating a love
that knows
no end

Just like a star
guiding the way
If from life's path
you ever should stray

The one, the only
to always depend
Your Mum
Your Saviour
Your Forever Best Friend

Rosalind Wood

Untitled

(In memory of a very dear friend killed in an air crash)

Tall dark stranger on a boat,
Our first awareness while afloat,
Introductions now we meet,
Shy eyes, lashes downwards sweep.
Fascination feelings new,
Two single people, me and you,
Joined together for a while,
The silence broken by a smile;
Our time together was too short,
But lengthened now, just by a thought.

Irene Ottaway

Evensong

Late April and the martins are here
darting and wheeling about the sky.
I have a special greeting for them
as I have for the pale narcissi
nodding and glimmering by the wall
where the first shadows begin to thicken.

The still-luminous sky, the blossom
sifting idly from the great gean trees,
the blackbird singing from the high roof ridge ~
these are the things that I remember
from our last far-off April evening.
Each year I bid them welcome in your name.

*'gean' tree is the wild cherry

May Marshall

Best Friend

Remember well with aching heart,
Of memories of that friendship past.
A true friendship that will never fade,
A friendship formed when very young,
To share all youthful things we need.
Those happy days when thought and dreams we shared,
We laughed, what fun we had.
Together always everywhere,
Whatever we had we always shared.
This friendship deep grows stronger still,
Even differences of opinion we shared.
To visit the local cinema,
To laugh out loud and share our views outside.
How natural did this friendship grow,
How stronger grew this bond.
Always there when hurt or ill,
And even through our teenage years,
This friendship never faltered.
But now my dear friend has gone,
And taken a part of me along.
But perhaps one day we'll meet again,
And let this friendship carry on.

Tom Usher

Afternoon Play

Two little old ladies
with little round hats
looked sharply, but smiled
like Egyptian cats.

Little red flowers
with tiny green leaves
in hands held hidden
made us two little thieves.

Brigitte Müller

A Friend In Need

'A friend in need'! ~ 'Is a friend indeed'!
An ancient maxim, folks, do heed.
This trusted proverb, bears some truth,
I learned this, from days, of my youth.

A life long friend, held in esteem,
Makes his appearance, when I dream.

At school, with homework, he helped me,
Whenever, he came round, for tea.
Then, after school, when out at play,
He used to keep bullies away.

Then ~ in the forces, still as pals,
We even, shared, each other's gals.

Then ~ in a trench, one night of 'hell',
The battle, did not go too well.
A mortar shrapnel, caught my thigh,
I really thought, that I would die.
My best friend, carried me away,
Or I, would not, be here to day.
He took me, to a 'First aid tent',
And then, ~ out of my life, he went.

What happened, is a mystery,
Though, I recovered, thankfully.

I never, saw my friend again,
Although, I searched form him, in vain.
Enquiries, came to a dead end,
Only, in dreams, I see my friend.
Then, he appears, persistently,
As 'Guardian Angel', guiding me!

Therefore:-   'A friend in need'! ~ it must be said;
              'Is friend indeed'! ~ Alive, or, dead!

A Rhymer

121

Haiku

You gave me a kiss.
I wish you'd loaned it instead,
And that I owed you.

Chris Moores

Mirror Of My Soul

I lived a generation long
    before your birth
Then lived another one before I knew
    you had been born
Not knowing that my soul had lacked
    its mirror of identity
Not knowing then that such a one
    could even be.

Sealed by a curtain of iron you learned so many tongues
    including mine
While I had learnt your language when in school
    and then forgot
But when we met, years, lands and languages
    became as one.

We cannot often meet, write once a month
Yet thoughts and feelings fly between
A thousand times each day.

To know as I am known
Be understood just as I understand ~
How can mere human words express
such trembling reality?

Harold Wonham

The Good Old Days

Come with me down memory lane and linger for a while.
Soon you will find that worried frown has changed into a smile.
Remember childhood playmates (now old alas like you),
The fun you had together ~ and yes the quarrels too.

Long days spent at the seaside, ice cream that donkey ride,
Candy floss, the rock pools where secret creatures hide.
Who built the best sandcastle with turrets oh so neat?
Then going home, a bag of chips, the perfect day complete.

Puppy love came suddenly, that wondrous rosy glow.
The secret dates, holding hands when at the picture show.
That first and tender stolen kiss, then parting at your gate,
The scolding from your parents for staying out too late.

This world we know and love, has changed in many, many ways,
But you'll agree without a doubt
'Those were the Good Old Days'.

Elsie MacKenzie

Tina

I remember your passion for charity shops
You took me around them all
We had carrier bags that were brimming
And we hardly spent anything at all!

We used to go 'round as a foursome
But the relationships crumbled to dust
We pondered the way of our future
Ours the one relationship we could trust.

You were always the life of the party
I envied the crowd you'd command
You travelled the length of the country
But in need you were always at hand.

We shared all our hopes and our dreams
Together we laughed and we cried
You gave me some wonderful memories
Although you were too young to have died.

I knew you were becoming discontented
Knew you searched for something more
You told me you loved me that last time
As I waved to you from my front door.

I couldn't believe you had done it
Your future had only just really begun
The news like a shot from a cannon
My world turned away from the sun.

I hope you are happy and safe now
I miss you more than you know
My best friend, I'll love you forever
I'm so sorry you felt you must go.

Julie Smith

Goodnight Everyone

Each night before I go upstairs
I pause to say some little prayers
To Ma and Da and Grandparents Hall
For all in the photos on the wall,
To brother Robbie and sister Jean
To a baby brother I've never seen
To our Blessed Lady, 'shining bright'
I smile, and wish them all 'goodnight.'

Mary Hall

How My Soul Hurts

How my soul hurts
My body aches
My mind overworks
My tears run dry
The time has come
For us to say goodbye
Kisses blown in the wind
Whispered words float
In the clouds
Sleep with winged dreams
Let your soul drift away
Remember good times
Smile
Rest in peace
My weary friend

Samantha Vaughan

Fadne

She cut a swathe through life,
Stippled with music and the sound of laughter,
As though the grass rejoiced.

Fame followed her fantasy writing,
Her witty contralto hypnotised bus queues!
Her love of the absurd wrinkled her nose
And filled lecture notes with jottings and ambiguous drawings.

Then one day the grass was sere,
The sounds strange hauntings ~
And she had gone;
Leaving behind memories and a son
In her image.

Eunice Barnett

From Yorkshire ~ With Love

'Twas on the way to Batley
I met this Yorkshire mum,
She got on the bus at Mytholmroyd
Going shopping with her son.

We laughed and chatted all the way
And hoped we'd meet again.
As they got off at Halifax
I knew I'd made a friend.

When I arrived home she phoned,
Inviting me for tea,
It felt like having 'the perfect mum'
'Cos Sheila cared for me.

Then just four weeks ~ to the day,
I couldn't believe my ears!
Her son rang on Thursday morn
To say his mum had died!

No words can ever quite express
The pain right through my heart,
I never thought how cruel life was
~ So soon we had to part!

She was so kind and gentle
Her eyes, were honest blue.
She understood my lonely life,
Her smile said, 'I love you!'

The time was short to share with her
We'd really only just met,
But all my days, that love will remain
From the mum, I'll never forget!

Blanche A Carson